Jenny's

99 Health Quotes
To Empower Your Life

First Edit

I0157749

Jenny Berkeley, RN, CHN

BESTSELLING AUTHOR

Jenny Berkeley, RN, CHN

Copyrights & Digital License

The purpose of this book and this series is to educate. It is sold with the understanding that the publisher and author shall have neither liability nor responsibility for any injury caused or alleged to be caused directly or indirectly by the information contained within this book. Where every effort has been made to ensure accuracy, the book's contents should not be construed as medical advice or a substitute for qualified medical advice. Statements regarding the nutritional content of foods were taken from a variety of sources and may be subject to change.

Each person's health is unique. Seek truth, seek a qualified professional to help guide you, but always follow your heart.

Publisher:
CM BERKELEY MEDIA GROUP
Ontario, Canada
First Edition

Digital ISBN: 978-1-927820-02-5
Print ISBN: 978-0-9811493-9-4

Copyright

Digital Edition License Notes

Holistic Health Nurse Series™ Books

Jenny created the **Holistic Health Nurse Series** as a flagship series to help not just patients, but other nurses, support staff, or health and wellness professionals. Her desire is that readers would see how common sense, logic, and modern knowledge of biology and nutrition can show where we all can put the right health habits to work for our long term benefit. Her personal motto: Good health is your birthright. Keeping it is your choice.

Volume 1: Eating4Eternity: Unlock Your Holistic Health Lifestyle™

If you feel that you are suffering prematurely from lifestyle diseases such as pain in the body, weight gain, constipation, tiredness, and what doctors call "getting old", then you need this book. It contains insights from Jenny, a nurse and health educator with over 23 years of experience in the medical profession. Her book will help you unlock that holistic health lifestyle that your body is aching for. Available in Print and Digital.

Volume 2: Sweet Raw Desserts: Life Is Sweet Raw™

This book contains some amazing desserts for anyone interested in the vegetarian and vegan diets. The recipes are rawfood recipes, which are created without cooking. Some of the recipes require a dehydrator which removes moisture from the food. These are healthier recipe options to their traditional, cooked counterparts. Available in Print and Digital.

Volume 3: Colon By Design: Overcoming the Stigma of Colon Sickness and Unlocking True Colon Health™
ISBN-13: 978-0-9868018-1-5

Jenny's passion for colon health has driven her to craft this excellent guide for anyone interested in keep their colon healthy. In the years to come, it is almost certain that this book will become the authority for ordinary people to turn to for health and wellness education. Available in Print and Digital.

Volume 4: Fresh Food4Life™: The Case For Taking Back Control of Your Food and Empowering Your Family and Community. ISBN-13: 978-0-9868018-2-2.

This next volume in the series takes a look at the most fundamental right of human beings on the planet. It is the right to have access to good quality food to eat and live. Available Exclusively on Amazon Kindle.

Volume 5: Jenny's 99 Health Quotes to Empower Your Life. ISBN-13: 978-0-9811493-9-4.

This 5th volume in the series is one that is close to Jenny's heart. This book is packed with quotes plus a meditation guide from Jenny. Jenny knows how patients can be scared, lonely, anxious, when in a hospital environment or even at home after receiving bad news. Jenny wants you to feel like she is right there with you holding your hand. Available Now. Ask your local bookstore for it..

Volume 6: Jenny's DETOX for Health ISBN-13: 978-1-927820-03-2.

This 6th volume in the series is focused on the holistic process of DETOXIFICATION. Jenny blends her medical background with nutritional background and spiritual insights to present a truly holistic guide on DETOX. People have been asking Jenny for this book and it is in the production pipeline. Look for this highly anticipated book is due for release in mid to late 2017.

Become a member of Jenny's website to get advanced knowledge of her upcoming books, tips, recipes, and more. Go to eating4eternity.org

* * * * *

Dedication

This book is dedicated to everyone who has experienced a setback due to disease or illness. For those of you who courageously and sometimes alone, face the scary fate before you, I dedicate this book to you. I have been there feeling it too, as you have.

I also dedicate this book to a few people who really make my life special because of their friendship and support. I dedicate this book to Eleanor W., Edgar W., Heather W., Lawrence W., Dawn V., Brian C., Anna-Maria C., Jerry Z., Daiva K., Guy D. and Imtiaz M.

Lastly I dedicate this book to my beloved husband and sons.

It is my hope that all my readers, like you, will benefit from the thoughtful words in this book.

* * * * *

Hi, I'm your holistic health nurse. I pop up periodically like this throughout the book with a helpful tip, trick, idea, or a story. This is not my only gig. I also appear in some issues of EternityWatch Magazine too. I know what you're thinking. I look like Jenny, correct? Well, I do look a bit like her but I'm the strict one. It is my pleasure to be your friend and companion as you journey through this book. See you soon!

Acknowledgements

This book, and indeed, this series would not have been possible without the hard work and dedication of all those who support the concepts of good health, a cruelty-free world, justice and equity, and love.

Writing one book is difficult enough, but writing a series of books is more consuming and challenging than a person realizes. Only another seasoned author truly appreciates the effort and the pain. Many writers have remarked that writing is an all-consuming mistress who desires no other competition for her attention. That seems so true at times.

On that note, I express my love and gratitude for all those on our team who keep the ship afloat and all do their parts to make this possible.

Jean Booth, our editor

CM BERKELEY MEDIA GROUP, our publisher

Dr. Brian Clement, my friend and mentor

My friends and family

Trusted Colleagues, our advanced readers

Thank you, all.

* * * * *

The Next Volume in the Series

This is the fifth book in the series. I decided to publish this book because of my belief that patients in the waiting rooms need some words of encouragement while waiting to see the doctor or waiting on a friend or loved one.

It is my hope that this book will become a standard fixture in hospital waiting rooms and clinics so that people can take a few moment to mediate and calm their body, mind, and spirit.

When I was pregnant with my first boy, I had a church friend Jane P. who was diagnosed with cancer. She was a single mom living in Canada and didn't have family members to accompany her to her treatments. I happened to work at the hospital where she was getting treatment so I would schedule my lunch around her chemo treatment and waddle my pregnant self down to meet her. When she saw me she would call out, "Jenny" with joy in her voice. I would hold her hand as she screamed in pain with the chemo going in her veins. I was glad I could be there for her during that lonely and scary time. Sadly, she passed on that year.

I hope this book I have written could be like me sitting there with you, holding your hand regardless of what you are going through; a broken leg, constipation, or cancer. I can't physically be there with you but my love is there with you as you read my book.

If you or a loved one is dealing with a dis-ease whether it is chronic or acute, keeping a copy of this book as your personal meditation book will help you stay calm.

My love and joy goes out to you in your moments of need.

* * * * *

Super Tip and Reminder

Did you know that Jenny has a special gift she is giving away to persons who purchase this book? Yes, it's true. After she created this book, she thought, there must be more she can do. So she came up with a gift for readers like you who purchased the book. Isn't she great? Yes, she is.

Anyhow, to get this gift, you have to go to her personal website at eating4eternity.org/bk5gift

You'll see the gift there plus details on how you can claim it for yourself. Go grab it immediately as I don't know how long she will keep it there.

Go to http://eating4eternity.org/bk5gift

Free Thank You Gift

Go to
http://eating4eternity.org/bk5gift

Table of Contents

* * * * *

Holistic Health & Wellness

Chapter 1

* * *

This chapter is not about the quotes but is about the mind of holistic health and wellness. You see, I was not always the holistic health and wellness nurse I am today.

I started out believing in the complete capability of the medical industry to fix whatever is wrong with the human condition. I had worked in all kinds of hospitals locally in Canada and internationally. I was greatly appreciated wherever I found myself working.

Then I got sick with my stomach. The pain was terrible and it was happening when I ate food and this pain would linger for hours afterwards.

At first it was mild discomfort so I ignored it. After a couple of years of ignoring it, it began to be more terrible than I could ignore.

I remember one time being at home and going into my walk-in closet closing the door and praying and crying out to God for help. I was honestly very scared. I had worked in the cancer ward and I had seen patients with stomach cancer. I was scared because I didn't want that to be me.

I had gone to the doctors to try to find out what was the problem. They did all the blood tests and the results came back negative. It seemed like my bloodwork was all good.

Yet my body was not lying. I was feeling pain every time I had food to eat. It was especially bad when I ate meat but I had not made the connection yet in my mind.

After years of dealing with the pain quietly, I met my husband. He didn't know I was having bad stomach pains but he was on a spiritual path of enlightenment. He had decided to wean himself off meats and dairy in order to increase his mental and spiritual focus.

By the time we got married, he had given up meat and dairy and I had given up meat. My pain was still present but not as severe. Over time, it was less but it never went away completely until I made a huge dietary change.

A series of events led me to the path which would eventually see me fully cured of my stomach pain. It has not returned in over 10 years. And I have become a champion of the holistic health and wellness approach to working with your body.

I run a successful magazine in Toronto reaching over 120,000 people each quarter. We bring the vegan and raw-vegan message to people who need to know about it. People who are suffering with their diseases that is a large part due to their diet and lifestyle. Our magazine, EternityWatch Magazine is available online at eternitywatchmagazine.com

And I have learned so much more since my marriage than in my previous years in the medical profession.

I see clients who are willing to invest in their own health and wellness. My fee is an investment in yourself and you get the best of both world with me. I am over 25 years in the medical profession so I know so many drugs, their effects, and interactions. I know medical protocols and processes. I know the industry like the back of my hand.

And I also know the holistic health side of the table. I know how eating rawfoods can help. I know what might potentially interact with a drug or medicine a person is taking. I know how to help my clients begin making the choices that will put them on the healthier path.

In addition to working with clients, I occasionally do workshops and lectures in the community. I am the author of five books and I have a few in the pipeline for release sometime in the near future.

I do this because I want to help patients. My love of people and my compassion for people is what led me to become a nurse. As a nurse, I care about people. I laugh with my patients, I cry with them, I feel when they feel. They are not a number to me. They are people.

I also have my strongly held beliefs in God. I have prayed many times for patients on the operating room(OR) table that God would help the patient and guide the surgeon's hand. Thank God, I have not had a patient die with me in the OR ever.

I had a close call one time where a patient was flatline and the room was a flurry of activity with people trying this and that to save the patient. It was taking a long time and they had exhausted all the medical means but I had one thing I would do for my patient. I went to my God to plead for his life to give him more time. Suddenly his heart began beating again. My God had heard my prayer and answered it for my patient.

There are physical limitations in the medical profession but I exist in the physical and the spiritual so I used every means available to me for my patients and clients. If you ever want to have me work with you, you can reach me through my website eating4eterity.org and click on working with Jenny.

* * *

People Are Important

Chapter 2

* * *

L ife is about the people we meet along this journey. Some of them are meant to test you, some to teach you, some to encourage you, and some for you to do likewise.

I've been blessed to meet some great people in my life and my Publisher Around and About section in the magazine always posts updates people can see. My readers tell me they are curious about what I'm up to.

This section, I'll post a few photos of the people I have had the joy and pleasure to have interacted with.

This photo is of me on television with Beverly Edward-Haines. Bev has been doing health in her church for years. When she started this TV program in Toronto and invited me on, I was glad to help her out.

I'm taking this photo of Arne and Ernestine, a husband and wife team bringing a really awesome product to Canadians. Pumpkinseed oil. They also support our work in the magazine.

Here's me above with some awesome seniors at the Zoroastrian Centre after a lecture I did for them. Seniors are the sweetest folks.

Here I am on television with Dr Lana Marconi talking about wheatgrass and sprouts. A few years later, I would be featured in a documentary movie she produced.

On the right, here's me with Health Canada whistleblower and author, Shiv Chopra.

Below, I'm with Kent and Lee, Brian Clement, and Anna Marie Clement.

On the left, me with Kris Carr, author of Crazy Sexy Cancer.

Below, I'm on TV again this time teaching people how to make a healthy superfood breakfast.

Above, promoting a plant-based diet at the hospital on an integrative health day.

Left, me with Victoras Kulvinskas Co-founder of Hippocrates Health Institute.

Above, me giving a lecture at the hospital for staff and patients

Right, me with Dr Joel Fuhrman. A nice guy and very knowledgeable too.

Above, promoting superfoods in a local healthfood store.

Right, me with Paul Nison in front of my wheatgrass and sprouts.

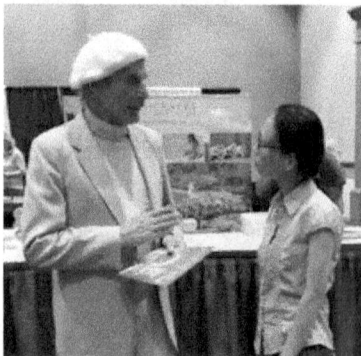

Above, at our annual rawfood event held in a local rawfood cafe.

Right, me with Dr Gabriel Cousens talking about medicine, health, and my magazine. :)

Jenny @ The Real Truth About Health Conference (Florida)

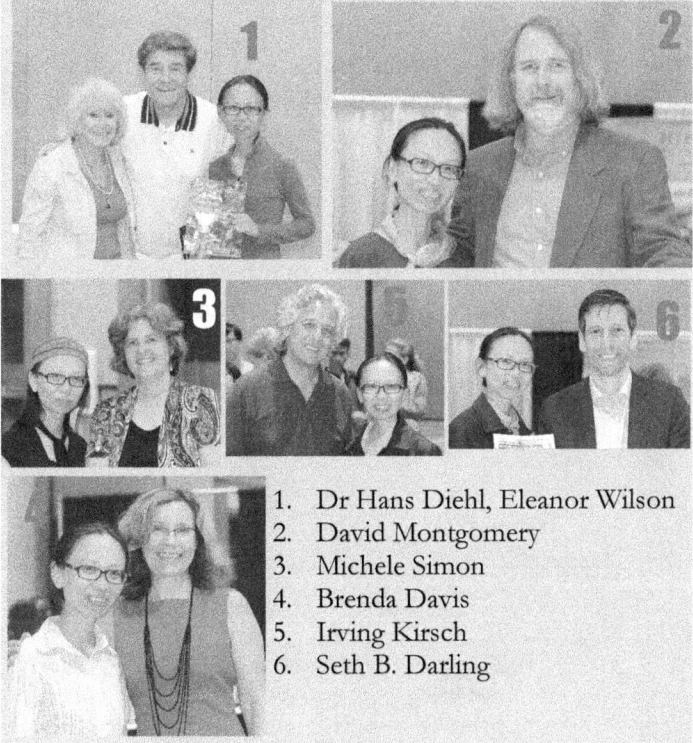

1. Dr Hans Diehl, Eleanor Wilson
2. David Montgomery
3. Michele Simon
4. Brenda Davis
5. Irving Kirsch
6. Seth B. Darling

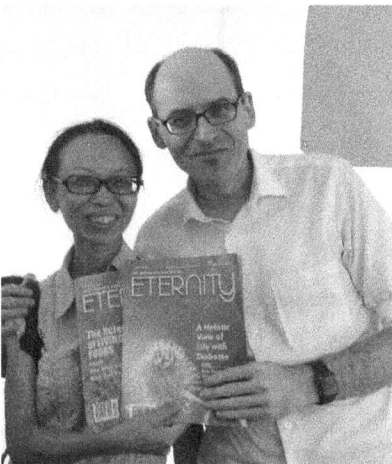

Above, hanging out at a conference and meeting all those wonderful people.

Left, me with Dr Michael Greger talking about medicine, health, and my magazine. :)

I could go on and on about the people in my life and the impact they have had on me. I can talk about the thousands upon thousands that I have had a chance to influence. But what I want to get you to focus on is that there are people in your life right now to inspire you, to motivate, to comfort you, and to pull you out of a negative situation.

Just look around you and you will see them. I hope you see that I am one of those persons too. As you are reading my book, you have an opportunity to have me with you in these pages too. Cherish the people in your life.

* * * * *

Super Tip and Reminder

People can be the best thing in your life. They can bring love, positive energy, and joy while being around. They can make you laugh or cry.

When you recognize the value of people, you appreciate the chances you have to spend precious time with them because time on this planet is limited.

Make a list of the people in your life and tell each of them personally how much they mean to you. It will mean a world to them and will help you feel great too.

Only when you are fully and satisfactorily informed then you give your consent.

Quotes On Illness

Chapter 3

* * *

The quotes in this section of the book are designed to help you think about the way in which you exist in relation to the world and the diseases in the world. I have worked in the medical industry, an industry that specializes in the dis-ease and illness. Having seen illness for more than two and a half decades, I have also seen patients and how they are impacted by these things. As you read the quotes in this chapter, take hope.

* * *

" Take a day to heal from the lies you've told yourself and the ones that have been told to you.

Maya Angelou, Activist, Author

Personal Meditation

When you see illness manifesting in your body, it is a signal to stop. It is time to retreat and meditate on the lies you tell yourself and the lies others tell you. It is time to do away with those lies and replace them with truth. Truth, like a healing salve will do wonders for your mind, body, and soul. Take the time you need whether it is a day, week, month, or year. Do it for you.

* * * * *

❝❝ As soon as we are fed unnatural processed foods, and we are conditioned by the media to believe incomplete or incorrect information about our choices, our health declines. It continues to do so from that point on.

Paul Nison, Author, Raw Food Chef

Personal Meditation

Understanding your illness includes making the connection that food may be related to the current state of your physical health. Illness may not be immediate like a cut or bruise. Illness may take time to develop slowly. And your food intake over time compared with the progression of your disease will tell you about your true state. Meditate on this quote quietly and think about the processed foods you eat daily.

* * * * *

❝ I spent 5 years searching for the correct homeopathic remedies to cure my asthma, but it wasn't until I found raw hygiene that I was able to stop my asthma attacks.

**Dr Tim Trader, Author,
Raw Food Advocate**

Personal Meditation

Sometimes it can take a person years to find what works for them in the fight with their dis-ease. The key is to never stop searching for that thing that will work. You also need to give your body time to heal itself. Meditate on whether you have been searching for answers or merely accepting non-answers.

* * * * *

❝ After more than two and a half decades in the medical profession, I am even more convinced now that patients need to be educated about the link between a vegan diet and optimal health.

**Jenny Berkeley, Nurse,
Certified Holistic Nutritionist, Author,
Magazine Publisher**

Personal Meditation

I love patients. I cry with them. I laugh with them. I listen to them. Over the years, I have seen more and more of them lacking the most basic knowledge of diet, nutrition, and health. My mission has been to help Canadians take back their health destiny through education. Meditate on your own knowledge. Are there things you need to learn?

* * * * *

❝ I was quite surprised to find my health, my attitude, my ability to stay on an even keel and my emotions, all improved dramatically when I went raw.

Dr Doug Graham, Speaker, Author, Raw Food Advocate

Personal Meditation

Graham started out with what he thought was a healthy state. When he switched to raw, he found a state of health even better than his previous assessment. Do you think you are healthy enough? Meditate on what good health looks like to you. How would your life improve if you could increase that level of good health even more?

* * * * *

❝ When we are born, we have the highest alkaline mineral concentration and also the highest body pH. From that point on, the normal process of life is to acidify. That is why degenerative diseases do not occur when you are young.

Sang Whang, Author

Personal Meditation

Your body is made up of 70% water. The normal processes of your body produces acid wastes even on a cellular level. The progression of disease is proportional to your accumulation of acidity on a cellular level. Meditate on whether you do anything to actively help your body regulate your pH.

* * * * *

❝ I couldn't believe it. Reality sank in with a jolt. I no longer had any breasts. Tears rolled down my face. The tears continued to drip down my cheeks making the pillowcase below my head damp. I closed my eyes but couldn't sleep. The pain was unbearable.

**Linda Morin, Author,
Hippocrates Alum,
Breast Cancer Survivor**

Personal Meditation

Linda wrote for us in EternityWatch a few years ago. Linda bravely fought her cancer. And in the quiet time alone in her hospital room, her heart broke at her loss of her breasts. All disease takes a toll on us individually, as a family, and as a community. Linda found Hippocrates Health Institute after her conventional therapies. She began her mind, body, soul healing journey at that time.

* * * * *

❝ I see parents come into the hospital with their children. They want to help their sick child but they themselves do not know how to secure good health. My passion is to help children by helping their parents understand key principles of good health.

Jenny Berkeley, Nurse, Certified Holistic Nutritionist, Author, Magazine Publisher

Personal Meditation

When I first started nursing, children did not get "diseases of old people." It would be a rare thing. Today children are getting high blood pressure, diabetes, obesity, heart disease and other older adult diseases. Meditate on your health and that of your children. Is there a way you could do more to help yourself and them? As a mother or father, are you giving them the best start you can?

* * * * *

❝ What we observe in dried blood (we use droplets of capillary blood from the top of the pinkie finger) are biochemical re-actions which leave cellular patterns that correlate with an anatomical and emotional history. From this we can gain extraordinary insights into the current functions and dysfunctions of the total physical person.

Dr Anna Maria Clement,
Author,
Co-Director, Hippocrates Health Institute

Personal Meditation

The history of a person is recorded in their blood. Modern live blood cell analysis can give us some clues. Meditate on what stories your blood might tell of your diet and lifestyle. Change your lifestyle and begin writing a new story in your blood and your cells.

* * * * *

> The art of medicine consists in amusing the patient while nature cures the disease.

Voltaire

Personal Meditation

There may have been truth to Voltaire's statement 100 or 200 years ago but sadly it is not so today. There are so many negative things that impact a patient's health concurrently that only a drastic change can allow God and natural healing processes to occur. This means that as a person suffering with a disease, you must make every effort possible to ensure the return of your good health.

This may involve hard work, discipline, and a lifestyle and dietary reformation. Patients are no longer amused. Neither can you afford to be.

Meditate on the things you need to cut out of your life to allow your mind, body, and soul to heal.

* * * * *

Never before in history has the human species been under such attack. Your cellular army, the immune system, constantly tries to decipher what new deviant is trying to invade your anatomy. You can imagine its exhaustion from the bombardment due to an untamed life of improper consumption. Nutrition is, without fail, the fundamental way that we build and rebuild healthy cells to create healthy organs and ultimately healthy people.

**Dr Brian Clement,
Co-Director, Hippocrates Health Institute**

Personal Meditation

Illness has become second nature to all of us. We are chronically exhausted from dealing with toxins in our air, our food, our water, and even via the electromagnet frequencies. To fight off disease, we must get back to the basics of proper nutrition. Meditate on this.

* * * * *

“ I'm an advocate for a holistic health plant-based lifestyle in the hospital environment. Nurses, doctors, support staff, all seem to find me in the hospital to get my advice. One doctor even joking told me he was not happy with the cafeteria menu and I should go down there and change it. I really love his comment as he has an open mind. I share what I know out of love for my colleagues and the great work we do for the Canadian healthcare system.

**Jenny Berkeley, Nurse,
Certified Holistic Nutritionist, Author,
Magazine Publisher**

Personal Meditation

Doctors and nurses are people too. They are doing their best in a high stress environment. Whenever a patient finds a doctor or nurse with a holistic approach, embrace them and support them. They are working to empower you and set you back in the driver seat.

* * * * *

There are good and bad people everywhere even in the medical system. The good ones have an open mind where disease and holistic health are concerned. They really want to help patients get better. There is a pandemic of sickness creeping over the world. I call it a coming health crisis Tsunami. Conventional hospital systems will not be able to cope with it. Doctors and nurses will suffer from burnout at that time. In order to prepare for this, it is up to you to educate yourself and your loved ones about the fundamental principles of being well.

Be a leader in your home and your community. The time is short and the need is great.

* * * * *

Super Tip and Reminder

Life is stressful with you are sick and going to visit your doctor or rushing to the emergence room. In all the stress, its easy to forget about informed consent, and simply sign a document given to you after a 30 second explanation. Don't. Informed consent is meant to protect patients and hospitals.

To protect yourself, take the time to ask lots of questions. If anything is unclear, ask for it to be explained better so you understand. The implications are life and death in some cases so you must know exactly what is happening and feel reassured that you are fully informed. Ask about side effects, chances of things going sour, risks, and any other question you need answered.

Only when you are fully and satisfactorily informed then you give your consent.

Quotes on Hope

Chapter 4

* * *

When we are in the hospital environment, we have to maintain a sense of hope. Hospital walls are drab and dreary. The smell is clinical and sanitized. It's easy to be distracted by the coldness of your environment and lose hope. I want you to refocus your mind and heart on hope. The quotes in this chapter will help you to do that.

* * *

Hope is the essence of the unseen. Within your body, it keeps you positive in the face of disappointment. It lifts your spirit when you are feeling discouraged. It helps you smile after you felt like crying. It is the most potent spiritual and mental component of your well-being. Never let anyone rob you of your hope. Keep it alive and nurture it daily. It will repay you thousands of times over.

**Vaughn Berkeley, MBA,
Author, Human Rights Award Winner
Co-Publisher EternityWatch Magazine**

Personal Meditation

Vaughn's right! Hope is not just some abstract idea. It is a fundamental part of your mental and spiritual life. Hope is what gives you the vision of the better life you deserve. When hope is extinguished, all reason to live is lost and you die even while you are alive. Meditate on ways to keep your hope alive.

* * * * *

> Thoughts of lack manifest as limitation. Thoughts of abundance manifest as success and happiness. Failure and success are but two ends of the same stick.

Ernest Holmes

Personal Meditation

Do you live in a life filled with lack or a life filled with abundance? Or maybe you live in a life of just-in-time. Our thoughts do shape our future and our destiny but most people don't believe. They wake up one day and say to themselves, "I'll be rich or famous." When it doesn't happen by the end of the day, they regard it as nonsense. But we are not magical genies to cause a single thought to materialize immediately. We are humans and we convert thoughts to actions and actions to outcomes. We plant seeds and reap at harvest time.

If you want a life of more abundance, then sow seeds of abundance today with a hope of reaping the abundance you seek tomorrow. I knew I would reach thousands upon thousands of people with a message of hope and health reform. I took action for years to make this dream a reality. Remember: think it, record it, work it, reap it. Do it all in hope.

* * * * *

❝❝ That which is built on alkalinity sustains: That which is built on acidity falls away – be it civilizations, human bodies, or the paper that preserves their knowledge.

Dr. T. Baroody

Personal Meditation

Ancient books were recorded in alkaline paper prior to 1850 when paper started being made with bleach, alum, and tannin, which are all acidic. Older books after the 1850 are disintegrating today. The best they can do is attempt to scan their pages to preserve them.

Are you bitter and acidic most of the times? Unhappy with life, your co-workers, or spouse, or children? These bitter/acidic thoughts are ruining your health and stealing your hope of a better future. You're burning out. Your digestive system will be ruined. Your body will feel like it's failing you on that path.

Replace bitterness of thought with acts of love and kindness. It's better for your health and your future. Find joy, peace, and contentment in the little things to keep your hope alive.

* * * * *

❝ I tell patients to never lose hope. I always am praying and hopeful in the operating room that God will look after the patient and guide the surgeon's hands. I pray for us all in there.

Jenny Berkeley, Nurse, Certified Holistic Nutritionist, Author, Magazine Publisher

Personal Meditation

My hope is part of my faith and belief in God. I pray in the operating room (OR) because I don't want any patient to die on the table. Thank God in my over two decades, no one has died on the table with me there. Some have come pretty close but God didn't allow death to take them. Everyone in the OR setting needs to hold on to hope as life and death are in the balance. Nothing is simply routine when the skin is punctured.

Meditate on those who have your best interest at heart. Their love and hope is a blanket of covering for you in your cold moments.

* * * * *

We move through this earth journey as primarily a spiritual entity, using human vehicles to study natural laws and vibratory realms of the universe.

Viktoras P. Kulvinshas
MS, Hipoocrates Health Educator
Co-Founder Hippocrates Health Institute

Personal Meditation

We are all on a journey of self discovery and self actualization. I love the way Viktoras says we are using human vehicles to study natural laws and vibratory realms. Imagine if you had kept your childlike curiosity alive instead of being caught up in day to day struggling to survive.

If we are here to learn and grow, how much have you learned up to this moment of your life? Have you learned the laws of gravity? Yes. Have you learned the sun sets in the west? Yes. Have you learned the laws which govern your body's optimal function? No? Well keep hope alive because if you are reading this book, life is affording you an opportunity to awaken your consciousness again. Seek and you will find, knock and the door will be opened, ask and you will receive. This is truth. Meditate on this.

* * * * *

" God promises us extraordinary health if we follow His commandments and listen to his voice. Unfortunately, we have broken nearly all of the age old health principles outlined in God's Word, the Bible.

Jordon Rubin, Author,
The Maker's Diet

Personal Meditation

Jordon makes a good point. Sometimes it feels like someone made a list of all the health principles and said, let's cause people to deliberately break them and study what happens. Being spiritual, I surround myself with people who understand the spiritual aspects of health principles. I learn and apply these principles in my life.

Meditate on how you can begin to learn these ancient health and wellness rules. If your church is not teaching it, then you need a coach who knows this stuff.

* * * * *

❝ The most sacred place isn't the Church, the Mosque or the temple, it's the temple of the body. That's where spirit lives.

Susan Taylor

Personal Meditation

Don't you know that your body is the temple of the Spirit of God; therefore honour your body with the works you do, the things you say, and the thoughts you think.

In this busy world, it is easy to forget this important truth. But you should remember it because your spirit is the root of all your healing. First, it must be healed of the things which bind it. And that healing starts with hope in God. Revive your spirit with thoughts of hope and acts of loving kindness.

Meditate on this and see how you can bring it to pass in your life.

* * * * *

"Ask, and it shall be given you; seek, and ye shall find; knock, and it shall be opened unto you: For every one that asketh receiveth; and he that seeketh findeth; and to him that knocketh it shall be opened.

The Book of Matthew, Chpt 7:7-8
The King James Bible

Personal Meditation

None of us have all the answers. Doubt is the enemy of hope. That is why these words are such encouragement. We should ask for wisdom, seek it out, and knock on the doors of those who will help us. There is a promise from God given by Jesus that we will be rewarded for our efforts in this regard. Take hope and take action.

* * * * *

" For me the answer is committing ourselves to a lifestyle that is totally in accord with the original plan. We cannot ignore science. Many great things are happening and will happen because of science but we cannot forget that nature is the ultimate science that was given to us by God.

**Dr Fred Bisci, author
60-year raw foodist,
Clinical Nutrionist**

Personal Meditation

Dr Bisci nails it! When we take the time to recognize and appreciate that our Creator is the inventor of human's original diet, we can search for clues in his writing and in nature about what works and what doesn't. As science continues to confirm what the deeply spiritual person already knows, we can find a renewed sense of hope for longevity and wellness.

* * * * *

> In a moment of decision, the best thing you can do is the right thing to do. The worst thing you can do is nothing.

Theodore Roosevelt

Personal Meditation

Decisions are choices. And choices have the ability to influence our lives in one way or another. Whether you decide to get up early to meditate or sleep in an extra 20 minutes, it will impact your life.

The same is true of hope. Whether you decide to be bitter and angry or hopeful and forgiving, it will impact your life. It will attract others around you who act the same way. One way or another you are obligated to decide. It is a duty of life on earth.

So will you choose hope today? Have you decided... Meditate on this concept for living.

* * * * *

> After I was born with neither arms nor legs, they [my parents] wondered what God had in mind in creating me. At first they assumed that there was no hope and no future for someone like me… Today, though, my life is beyond anything we could have imagined.

Nick Vujicic
Motivational Speaker, Author of Life
Without Limits

Personal Meditation

Nick was born with no arms and legs. That is a low starting point in life but God has used him to give hope to millions of people. He travels across the world speaking of God's love and motivating others to live in hope. I want you to consider your life now and let your experience give those closest to you hope. Meditate on how you can use your circumstances to bring hope to someone.

* * * * *

If you want radical change in your life, you're only going to get it by renewing your mind. The old mind with the old ways of thinking and seeing is ill equipped to take you forward in this journey.

Vaughn Berkeley, MBA
Magazine Publisher, Microfinance
Consultant, Founder of An Online Learning
Academy, Author of Break The Poverty
Curse

Personal Meditation

Vaughn's love of life includes his love of people and desire to bring hope to others. Your old way of thinking has gotten you here. Hope is the seed you need to help you change your ways of thinking and seeing the world. That change brings new hope and more changes. The cycle goes on and on until you are a new creature formed in love and hope. Meditate on the steps to changing your thinking and your behaviours.

* * * * *

> To be beautiful inside and out is our natural human state. When we admire sparkling eyes, fabulous skin, and lustrous hair, what we're admiring is the teamwork of a healthy liver, colon, kidneys - a completely functional set of organs, skin included.

Tonya Zavasta
Author, Rawfood Coach
beautifulonraw.com

Personal Meditation

Tonya's a beautiful woman, inside and out. I heard her speak in Toronto when I was new to my rawfood journey. She spoke of her difficult childhood dealing with her disability. Her painful surgeries and recovery. Her desire to get well and how rawfood has helped her. Her insights into being beautiful on raw are very good. Most of all, her faith in a good God who loves and cares for his children. Meditate on the quote from her and see how fundamental it is.

* * * * *

“ Babies held mostly against mother's body feel safe and right in the world, a feeling that, like breastfeeding, is a continuation of life in the womb. It makes a lot of sense to hold baby skin-to-skin, as cortisol, the stress hormone, is reduced when baby feels safe and secure against the mother's skin, and the love hormone, oxytocin, is increased.

Karen Ranzi, MA
Author, Rawfood Coach
superhealthychildren.com

Personal Meditation

Karen talks about how holding your child reduces your stress hormone and increases your love hormone. Adults need to be around their children and grandchildren. Meditate on if you are spending enough time with your young children or grandchildren.

* * * * *

> ❝ I eventually opened the first Montessori school there in our home. There were 16 children in attendance and only 5 of them spoke English! The rest spoke Arabic, German, French and Italian… In about 3 months all the children spoke English!… Isn't that an amazing testament to the power of a child's mind?

Eleanor Wilson
Hippocrates Health Educator,
Montessori Teacher/Principal

Personal Meditation

Eleanor has written for us in EternityWatch before. She is an amazing 80+ young woman and an inspiration to me. She always has a word of encouragement or some wisdom from her experiences in life. Speaking about the power of the mind, you see a child can learn a 2nd language without effort. But the mind is much more powerful than that. Develop your childlike curiosity for the world around you. Experience everything as if it were new to you.

* * * * *

❝ We must be patient with each other. Patience is a virtue. It is something that quiets the storm raging in the hearts and minds of others. It is a rock which cannot be beaten by the waves of chaos.

**Jenny Berkeley,
Nurse, Certified Holistic Nutritionist,
Author, Magazine Publisher**

Personal Meditation

Sometimes I've seen people in the hospital behave so impatiently. It could be doctors, nurses, support staff, or even patients. And I've seen a patient person get to the root of the matter and calm the situation. When the situation become confrontational, it creates added stress for everyone in an already high stress environment. Meditate on how many times in a week or day you lose your patience. Consider ways to help you remain patient should those situations arise again. Your calm and patience might be the hope that someone around you is looking for at that very moment.

* * * * *

You know why my patients and clients like me? Because I am patient with them. Long ago I recognized that people are normal people; they hurt, they feel frustrated, they feel sad, or angry. I learned to use patience to listen to their expressions of cries for help. Then we are able to work out a solution that is a win-win or at the very least the patient or client will feel secure in the knowledge they have as to why something was not possible. They know that I would have tried my best. If I can help give someone a renewed sense of hope, I have moved them significantly along the path of a better life.

* * * * *

Super Tip and Reminder

There are folks who are perpetually angry or ill-tempered. Do not spend time with them as it will cause you to learn their bad habit.

You see, emotions are contagious. Normally, a person who is always filled with anger and rage will eventually cause you to be infected by it. The only exception is for those who are connected to the divine nature given to us by God. Those people can teach an angry person calm, patience, and love because their stronger influence is from heaven.

If you see angry people around your life, change your environment and hang out with people who have calm, patience, and a sense of hope. You will learn this and it will benefit you.

Quotes on Raw Living Foods

Chapter 5

* * *

The quotes in this section along with the personal meditation will help you to focus on the importance of a living food diet. I discovered this when I was sick. An elderly couple gave me a book which started me on the journey. They prepared rawfoods for me to try at their home. It starts with someone telling you what you did not know. As you read these and the meditation, take time to meditate on your own life.

* * *

Green is the natural way of life and the only true superfood on the planet Earth. From the SOIL all the way to the SUN up above, combine the two and what do you get? GREEN! We need to reconnect to the Earth, to listen to nature's wisdom and allow our bodies to heal. It's time to become healthy again by tapping into the basic yet profound awareness of our instincts.

**Michael Bergonzi,
Wheatgrass Aficionado**

Personal Meditation

The green juices of grasses are foundational building blocks of our health and wellness. Going back to the grass is tapping into the energy of the earth and the sun and the vibration of life on the planet. Meditate on how to reconnect with your body, your health, your planet, with a refreshing glass of green juice.

* * * * *

Your physical, emotional, and spiritual state affect your health. A high raw diet, 70% or more of nutrient dense raw foods will ease the physical burden of digestion allowing you to focus more on the emotional and spiritual wellness.

Jenny Berkeley, Nurse, Certified Holistic Nutritionist, Author, Magazine Publisher

Personal Meditation

The raw food diet is not a cure-all because food is not the only thing that affects us. However, it is a major thing after breathing. You eat every day of your entire life. So you have many opportunities to improve your diet during the course of your lifetime.

Meditate on how you can start adding more raw, ripe fresh fruits and veggies to your diet daily.

* * * * *

[At 72] I am at peace with the knowledge that no matter how well I take care of myself, one day my life's cycle will end. I do not, however, spend time contemplating the end. Instead, I focus on the now – living well and living life to the fullest are pivotal, and I want people to know that they, too, are capable of being psychologically, physiologically, and spiritually sound at any age. The power is within us, but we must take the necessary steps to implement that power.

**Annette Larkins,
30 Raw Vegan Lifestyle, Author**

Personal Meditation

Annette is a wonderful example of a living food lifestyle in contrast to her husband of many decades. He looks his age while she looks 40-50 years old. Annette is 70+ years old. Her spirit and vitality have never diminished while feeding her body what it needs to thrive. You can begin feeding your body a living food, raw-vegan diet too.

* * * * *

❝ As soon as healing takes place, go out and tell someone else

Maya Angelou, Activist

Personal Meditation

This is exactly what happens in the rawfood/living foods movement. People switch over to a high raw diet or 100% rawfood diet and see tremendous benefits in a relatively short space of time. Then they come back home and tell their loved ones. Then they tell their neighbours and friends.

Some people go on to start businesses, run coaching classes, blog about their experience and more. It's like the parable of the woman who searches all over her house for a missing coin. When she finds it, she tells all her friends about it.

And it's like that with eating more raw foods. When you find out how good the food tastes, how beneficial it is to your body, how guilt free your eating becomes, you naturally want to tell those around you. So why not give it a try or look for someone who has. They will surely tell you about their experience.

* * * * *

> The transformation of lifestyle got me so hooked that I started my own business where I encourage people to live healthier and be their own guide in making changes.

Sandra Maes,
Rawfood Chef, Instructor & Coach

Personal Meditation

Is your lifestyle inspiring you to get out and tell others about it? If not, then is your lifestyle something that leaves you tired, dreading Monday mornings, longing for Fridays, and overall just being unsatisfied?

That's not living a good life. That's struggling to survive. Maybe it's time you open your heart and mind to a lifestyle change that really makes you excited to be alive again.

* * * *

> Live foods give the power of unbroken wholeness in our food. The wholeness of live foods is not only health-producing but also non-reproducible by technology, which tends to fragment nutrition.

**Gabriel Cousens,
MB, MD(H), ND(hc), DD,
Author, Teacher, Founder of Tree of Life
Center**

Personal Meditation

Living foods are at their very best, a source of nutrition directly from the earth. It is pure and unadulterated by human processing. The purity and wholeness of that food brings what you need to feed your body. How much of your daily diet consists of raw living foods? Meditate on your own diet and consider how you can improve it.

* * * * *

I took it upon myself to learn about food and the relation to wellness. I discovered food as one of the most powerful tools in maintaining wellness and vitality. Our body is wonderfully made and it is made to process high quality nutrition in order to give us health and vitality.

Jenny Berkeley, Nurse, Certified Holistic Nutritionist, Author, Magazine Publisher

Personal Meditation

My journey on the path to holistic wellness only began once I got sick and the medical industry was unable to help me. I found the answer in living foods. And from there found so many other truths about life. Meditate on this point and consider how living foods can help you.

* * * * *

> In the beginning living foods seem bland and uninteresting because our tastes were previously unnaturally stimulated. When you give your body time to adjust to the real taste of foods, your body naturally craves the goodness of it all.

Vaughn Berkeley, MBA
Magazine Publisher, Microfinance
Consultant, Founder of An Online Learning
Academy, Author of Break The Poverty
Curse

Personal Meditation

Vaughn tells it like it is from an honest point. At first, you might resist the tastes and sensations of living foods because your body is conditioned to crave highly processed foods. But in a short space of time, you will be amazed by the way your body embraces the raw-vegan living food lifestyle. Meditate on how you can start today. Begin with fresh apples, or other fresh fruit.

* * * * *

❝ Despite the diversity of approaches to raw food, there are many common benefits people are looking to achieve by eating this way. Three of the most notable would include high water content, nutrient content, and lower calorie density.

**Dr Karin Dina, DC,
Author, Researcher, Clinician**

Personal Meditation

Karin shares an interesting point here. Though many people may suggest different approaches to the rawfood lifestyle, there are essentially three common benefits we can always get. Meditate on whether you are currently getting these three benefits and how to increase them in your life.

* * * * *

> And God said, Behold, I have given you every herb bearing seed, which is upon the face of all the earth, and every tree, in the which is the fruit of a tree yielding seed; to you it shall be for meat.

God's Words To The First Man and Woman, The Book of Genesis, Chapter 1, Verse 29, King James Bible

Personal Meditation

We see from the holy scriptures that the diet for humans is fruits and herbs, and plant-based. There were no animals foods or animal products. There were no highly processed foods, preservatives, additives, and other stuff. It was meant to be all natural. How far away humanity has drifted. Meditate on how you can align yourself with the divine guideline for a healthy diet.

* * * * *

> Feeding your family more raw foods doesn't have to be difficult. Start with foods your family normally enjoys - foods that are visually appealing, taste great, and are familiar and comforting.

Cherie Soria
Rawfood Chef, Author, Founder of the
Living Light Culinary Institute

Personal Meditation

Cherie is a wonderful person who has written for us in the magazine many times. Her living light institute has helped many people become raw-food chefs and take their living food experience to the next level. When you know the benefits of this lifestyle, you may decide to tell and teach others. The good news is difficult to keep to yourself when you want to help others. Meditate on if there are people in your life who know about this or can help you. Seek out people like me, Jenny, who are boldly helping others.

* * * * *

Hospital food is awful. Thankfully times are changing. I've seen some leading edge hospitals in the USA with their own greenhouses that provide fresh salads to the patients daily. Hopefully Canadian hospitals will see the cost savings and health benefits of this and implement it.

Jenny Berkeley, Nurse, Certified Holistic Nutritionist, Author, Magazine Publisher

Personal Meditation

I have been involved in two events at my hospital promoting a holistic approach to wellness. I believe the leadership is a big part of this initiative. More living foods are beneficial for us all. Patients can also do their part to encourage hospitals to grow salad gardens for patients. Meditate on how you can get involved in this with your local hospital.

* * * * *

> The consistent interplay of the spirit and emotions is as essential to life as eating; it is likely more important.

**Dr Brian Clement,
Co-Director, Hippocrates Health Institute**

Personal Meditation

Brian touches on an interesting point here. Eating is essential to life. And so is the connection with the spiritual and the emotional. Food feeds our body while the rest of life feeds our mind and soul. The living food diet and lifestyle is one that helps to nourish us on all three of those levels. The living foods bring clarity and remove the fogginess in the brain. With this clarity, we perceive our world in truth and our emotions are now truly aligned with who we are. Meditate on how to become your true self on this journey.

* * * * *

Food is love. Food is survival. Think about it. When we are born, we are fed by our parents out of the great love our mothers and fathers have for us.

**Dawn Vickery,
Entrepreneur, Founder of Raw Elements**

Personal Meditation

Dawn is a dear friend of mine. She is passionate about helping other Canadians get access to high quality superfoods. She has written for us and is an incredibly happy and joyful woman. In her presence you can't help but smile. Her love of food shows and she makes a good point. The kind of dead food people eat is void of love. Living foods are love infused. Superfoods are high nutrients. Feed yourself the best because you love your body.

* * * * *

Switching to a raw-vegan/living food diet changed my life. I might even say it saved my life because it was the genesis of a new direction in my focus and mission in life. Yes, I as sick. Yes, I was scared. But from that point in my life, I have become a champion of the movement. I have gone on to reach more people in life, literally hundreds of thousands of people. You can't expect living foods to undo year of damage you've been doing to your body after you eat that way for 2 or 3 weeks. But, you can begin the process and with time, your body will replace old sick cells with newer healthier cells. Find a coach to work with you to help you understand the journey.

* * * * *

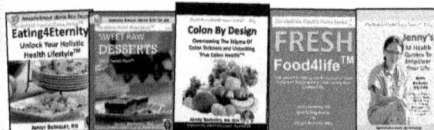

Quotes on Veganism / Vegetarianism

Chapter 6

* * *

The quotes in this section along with the personal meditation will help you to focus on our relationship to the animals and the foods we eat. Consciousness is when you awake from the sleep which envelops the majority of society. As you read these and the meditation, take time to meditate on your own life and the impact you are having.

* * *

" This war on animals, killing an estimated 75 million animals daily in the U.S. alone, is the underlying war driving our war on other humans, the Earth, less-privileged people, wildlife, and, ultimately, ourselves. It is vast and invisible, and yet everyone, except for vegans, is participating in it, and with dollar votes, demanding it to continue. Until we understand that purchasing and eating animal foods is also a form of cold violence, we will as a culture, never be more than merely ironic in our quests for peace, justice, freedom, health, and wisdom.

**Will Tuttle,
Author of The World Peace Diet**

Personal Meditation

How do you participate in the culture of cruelty? Are you making choices with your precious shopping dollars that support peace and harmony or that support violence and disharmony. You are a spiritual being in a flesh body. Meditate on the impact participating in this violence has on your spirit.

* * * * *

With all the heavy animal foods, always indigestibly combined with processed carbohydrates (the usual junk and party fare) that are typically offered at holiday time, children, whose bodies and brains are still developing, are more prone to getting sick.

Karen Ranzi, MA
Rawfood Author, Coach

Personal Meditation

Karen has written for us numerous times in the magazine. She is a knowledgeable woman. During the holidays, parents stuff their kids with unhealthy foods. It's time to break with tradition. Meditate on how to make a positive impact on meals during the holidays.

* * * * *

> Today we can produce enough vegetarian food to feed everybody in the world. We don't need to kill animals.

**Dr. Janez Drnovsek, (Vegan)
2nd President of Slovenia**

Personal Meditation

President Drnovsek is no doubt a learned man as he has his doctorate. And to become a head of state one must understand the matters of state. His insights into the true nature of food on this planet is very true above. Only by giving up the flesh of animals, can be use the space to properly feed humans with a plant-based diet. Ponder on this.

* * * * *

This century will elevate nutrition to a place of prominence in health restoration. Led by a pioneering international group of orthomolecular doctors, there is mounting research and growing evidence that nutrients that build the strength of one's anatomy are, ultimately, the best way to prevent and heal disease. Hippocrates Institute stands as a perfect example supporting this evolving science. The time has come for us to use common sense and once again realize that before modern science existed, the inherent tapestry of life was woven with simple, natural processes including the consumption of nutritious food.

**Dr Brian Clement,
Co-Director, Hippocrates Health Institute**

Personal Meditation

Science is catching up to history. Thankfully in the minds of progressive medical and holistic practitioners, we see more enlightenment about the natural truth: Let thy food be thy medicine. Meditate on whether you food has been the source of your medicine or the source of your sickness.

* * * * *

> I have personally experienced many miracles in my own life after adopting a vegan diet 17 years ago. I love to share different ways God has healed me and I also love to hear from others their personal recovery stories because it helps motivate me to continue on this path and stay in tune to what I have found to be true.

Andrea Nison
Mother of two daughters, blogger, vegan

Personal Meditation

Andrea has written for us in the magazine over the years. She's a wonderful lady and a dear friend. Her faith helps to fuel her passion for this lifestyle. How can your faith help you to adopt a living food diet or vegan diet? Doing what is right for your body, the planet, and your loved ones is the correct option. Meditate on your path on this journey.

* * * * *

We can turn things around, but we have to go to the roots – to the food program—and effectively deprogram ourselves. This means effectively questioning the official stories about protein, calcium, and everything else relating to nutrition, and exploring the deep structure of healthy living. As we extend love, freedom, and health to nonhuman animals, hungry people, workers, and future generations, we sow the seeds of joy, harmony, and wellness in our lives, and bless everyone.

**Will Tuttle,
Author of The World Peace Diet**

Jenny's Personal Meditation

Vegan is the dietary choice and lifestyle option of conscious thinkers because it demands that people question the old misinformation, explore for themselves, and find the truth based on today's knowledge and understanding. It means taking personal responsibility for your health and the larger implications of your dietary and lifestyle choices.

* * * * *

For as long as men massacre animals, they will kill each other. Indeed, he who sows the seed of murder and pain cannot reap joy and love.

**Pythagoras,
Greek mathematician**

Personal Meditation

If love and joy is what you want for yourself and your family, you've got to sow seeds of peace and love. While you partake in the murder of animals, when unnecessary, you are sowing seeds of suffering, murder, and chaos. Stop being part of the problem and become part of the solution. Choose a vegan diet and sow seeds of joy in a free and clear conscience.

* * * * *

A vegan diet is a great starting point and a raw food vegan diet full of a wide spectrum of healthy fruits, vegetables, sprouts, and greens can be another very useful tool in helping MDs achieve such goals [getting rewarded for patients getting healthier] for a healthy Canadian population.

**Jenny Berkeley, Nurse,
Certified Holistic Nutritionist, Author,
Magazine Publisher**

Personal Meditation

Back in 2012, I wrote an article about doctors in Cuba who were compensated based on their ability to get patients on a healthier lifestyle. They got bonuses for getting patients to reduce their BMI, or Blood pressure, or quit smoking, or other healthy lifestyle choices. If Canadian doctors were given such rewards, we'd see more efforts being made to get people into healthier lifestyles. And a plant-based diet is a great way to get healthier. Meditate on how you could switch to a vegan diet since you will have to do it for your health.

* * * * *

Unless we change our food choices, nothing else matters. Because it is meat that is destroying most of our forests. It is meat that pollutes our waters. It is meat that is creating disease which leads to all of our money being diverted to hospitals. So, it's the first choice for anybody who wants to save the Earth.

**Maneka Gandhi,
Indian Parliament Member**

Personal Meditation

Maneka very eloquently states what is a global crisis. People are making poor food choices which make them sick and cause them to spend too much trying ti recover their health. It's better and cheaper to go for prevention rather than treating the disease.

* * * * *

Education is your passport to the future, for tomorrow belongs to the people who prepare for it today.

Malcolm X

Personal Meditation

Have you taken the time necessary to educate yourself about the horrors of the meat, dairy, and fish industries? Do you know the deplorable conditions of these sick and infested pieces of flesh people eat and call it meat? An education in veganism is necessary to stand up for what is right AND to preserve your body temple from things which lead to sicknesses and diseases.

Some of the brightest minds are now advocating a plant-based diet for health and longevity. If you want tomorrow to truly be yours, then educate yourself today about the benefits of a plant-based lifestyle.

* * * * *

❞ I never see an egg brought to my table but I feel penetrated with the wonderful change it would have undergone but for my gluttony; it might have been a gentle useful hen, leading her chickens with a care and vigilance which speaks shame to many women.

St. John de Crevecoeur (1735-1813)

Personal Meditation

Meat, eggs, dairy, and fish, demand the life a living sentient being. Eggs are made by hens caged for their natural lives and when they are spent, they are used for food.

When did people become "consumers" that devour without self control. It is up to you to switch off the consumerism mindset and become a human being which manifests love, light, and joy to all those beings around you. You deserve to be the best you were meant to be.

* * * * *

When I went vegan it was cold turkey. I was already sick with my stomach and so drastic change was necessary for me. In that sense, I'm thankful for the awakening that resulted from my paying attention to myself in my illness.

Jenny Berkeley, Nurse, Certified Holistic Nutritionist, Author, Magazine Publisher

Personal Meditation

The plant-based diet was the one necessary for me. And though I did not know it, it would lead to my awakening to the horrors of the meat industry. The illness was a wake up call. My health and well being was the purpose. And the path has led me towards a more responsible way of living on earth without contributing to the needless suffering of animals for food. You can be a part of a socially responsible movement too.

* * * * *

> We cannot demand more each year from the soil or from a cow, or expect a chicken to grow in half the time it would naturally do: they are not machines, they are living things, and their natural mechanism, if it breaks down, cannot be repaired like an industrial milling-machine.

Carlo Petrini, Author
Slow Food Nation

Personal Meditation

Carlo tells us here that we as individuals and as a society are placing unreasonable demands on food animals. Veganism is the peaceful, mindful, and responsible way.

* * * * *

Don't let the holidays compromise your health. As you learn to create new holiday traditions, you'll thrive and be a good example to friends and family as they join you in celebrating the season of good cheer.

Cherie Soria,
Rawfood Chef, Author, Founder of the
Living Light Culinary Institute

Personal Meditation

Cherie's point about the holidays are very insightful. You see, holidays are a time when people can fall off the vegan or rawfood wagon. Under the peer pressure from family members, people compromise on their diet. Instead of compromising why not be a leader among those who love you. I have influenced hundreds of thousands of people around Toronto with my magazine and books. I influence my family, friends, and clients. I want to encourage you to stand strong for your plant-based diet and lifestyle. You can be a light in the darkness.

* * * * *

> If I could to do the right things correctly, I would only wish that I had learnt those things as early as possible in my life. Failing that, I'd start learning them right away.

Vaughn Berkeley, MBA
Magazine Publisher, Microfinance Consultant, Founder of An Online Learning Academy, Author of Break The Poverty Curse

Personal Meditation

Vaughn makes an excellent point. The best time to learn the right way is when you are young. However, if you missed that opportunity, then now is the next best time. Diet changes, lifestyle changes, changes in your system of beliefs are all possible given the right access to knowledge and the right coach or guide to encourage you. A raw-vegan diet is exciting, new, and worth the effort when you do it correctly.

* * * * *

❝❝ More people talk themselves into failure than talk themselves into success.

Zig Ziglar
Author, Motivational Speaker

Personal Meditation

I've heard people say, "Oh I could never do that," or "I could never give up meat or dairy." You see these people have already talked themselves into failure before they even began. Sometimes you do that too. We all do at times. It's only when an external factor is more powerful than your internal negative self-talk that you get up and get into action because failure is not an option. Meditate on this. How many times in a day or week do you use negative self talk. Record it in journal and see for yourself just how much you are defeating yourself.

* * * * *

I went raw-vegan at first because of my sickness and my deep desire to heal my body from the inside out. Then after a few years on that path, I discovered veganism, and the connection between the pain and suffering of animals used in the food industry. Billions of animals are mercilessly slaughtered every year to feed human's perverted appetites. A plant-based diet is the original and best diet for the human being. Veganism is a lifestyle with diet being one component of that lifestyle.

* * * * *

Super Tip and Reminder

It's okay to make mistakes and stumble along the path of your life-change spectrum. You may decide to go vegan but struggle with your addiction to dairy. Don't give up. Educate yourself more and more about the sickness, disease, blood and puss, and other harmful aspects of it.

You may go raw-vegan and only be able to do a 50% level at first. Don't be discouraged. Keep at it and over time, your cells will adjust. Just be persistent and vigilant. Don't put yourself in the pathway of temptation.

You can do better. You owe it to yourself.

Quotes on Mental Health

Chapter 7

* * *

The quotes in this section along with the personal meditation will help you to focus on the things in your life that are important. Relationships are not formed only with people. There are relationships to things we develop over time or to habits we develop. As you read these and the meditation, take time to meditate on your own life and relationships.

* * *

An indescribable feeling never known before of better health, more vital energy, better efficiency, and more endurance and strength came to me and gave me great joy and happiness just to be alive. This was not only of the physical, but there was great change in my mental ability to perceive, to remember, greater courage and hope, and above all an insight into the spiritual which became like a sunrise, throwing light upon all higher and spiritual problems.

Professor Arnold Ehret
Author, Mucusless Diet Healing System

Personal Meditation

Your mental state, and clarity of thought is impacted by illness or health. When you are health, you naturally take for granted your mental state and only the onset of sickness causes you to realize what you lost. Professor Ehret highlights what happens when it regained after a serious illness. It is like sunlight bursting into darkness. Your own experience can be magnificent. Meditate on how much you want or need that experience and decide to do what it takes.

* * * * *

> The good and the bad have shown their merchandise, ultimately I must make the choice,
> I have a plan if I can of course.
> Carry it out to end my troubled heart,
> Why sit and wait at the gate of the cruel world for a benefactor to arrive?

**Poem of Hazif of Shiraz,
Ancient Persian Poet
Translated by Nader Khalili**

Personal Meditation

The poet reminds the reader that the world presents both the good and the bad as fruits of the season. Nothing is hidden or secret for long. Ultimate it comes down to your personal choice, whether you will choose the good or the bad. The poet reminds us that is is pointless to wait on some benefactor but we should get up and make the choice so that we may partake of the reward. This sums up my motto: "Good health is your birthright, keeping it is your choice." Choice begins in the mind and spirit. Make yours today.

* * * * *

The mental health of patients are important in daily living. Excessive moodiness, depression, anxiety, and overall lethargy are signs of nutritional imbalances, and a holistic lifestyle imbalances. Fixing it requires multiple interventions but all are possible with professional help.

**Jenny Berkeley, Nurse,
Certified Holistic Nutritionist, Author,
Magazine Publisher**

Personal Meditation

When you feel out of whack and your coping mechanism are failing you on a daily basis, then this is already a warning sign that you whole self needs an intervention. There could be many things rooted in your weakened mental state but help is possible and victory is possible. Meditate on your life and see if you've been "losing it," that is, exercising poor coping skills or excessively moody. Help is possible. Choose to seek it and receive it with gratitude.

* * * * *

"Along the way, it has become obvious that the diet changes my research team found to promote physical health and those that other researchers have found to be critical for brain health are remarkably similar. Specific foods and eating patterns have an powerful protective effect.

**Dr Neal Barnard,
President, Physicians Committee for
Responsible Medicine**

Personal Meditation

Your brain in part of the system known as the human body. It is connected to the body and operates within the system. Therefore it is important to note that a diet that leads to peak physical health will also have a positive impact on the brain. And a brain that is properly nourished and free of pollution will be clear to perceive greater things, to connect with the divine, and to guide your intellect to higher purposes.

* * * * *

❝ I purpose in my day to be happy and optimistic. Why? Because it is a much more pleasant company to attend. Do I feel worried or anxious? At times, but I chase it away quickly out of my mind as I have no desire to entertain such unwanted brain-mates. Hold strong what is good and right and reject that which you know to be wrong. That's all.

**Vaughn Berkeley, MBA,
Author, Human Rights Award Winner
Co-Publisher EternityWatch Magazine**

Personal Meditation

Vaughn chooses happiness and optimism to start his day. It helps put things into perspective throughout the day. It sets the tone and vibrations for your day. When you wake up each day without making that choice, then you are simply letting life happen at random to you. Why not take control instead? Choose to be happy and optimistic today and everyday.

* * * * *

If you can disentangle yourself from your selfish self, all heavenly spirits will stand ready to serve you
if you can finally hunt down your own beastly self, you have the right to Solomon's kingdom
you are a blessed soul who belongs to the garden of paradise, is it fair to let yourself fall apart in a shattered house? You are a bird of happiness in the magic of existence, what a pity you let yourself be chained and caged,
but if you can break free from this dark prison named body, soon you will see you are the sage and the fountain of life.

**Poem of Rumi,
Ancient Persian Poet
Translated by Nader Khalili**

Personal Meditation

It is time to set your mind free from the prison of the physical. Allow your mind to soar. Think thoughts of the holy and divine. Live life and become the beauty of life. It begins with your mindful and purposeful choice

* * * * *

> They [My children on earth] know nothing, neither do they understand; they walk in darkness; all the foundations of the world are out of course. I have said, 'you are gods; and all of you are children of the most high [God],' but you shall die like men and fall like one of the princes [of this world].

**Excerpt from Psalm 82,
The Holy Scriptures
Authorized King James Version**

Personal Meditation

Imagine what it is like to be a child of god. Imagine a brain of immense intellect. Imagine a life of love and compassion. Your mind makes this possible or impossible. Choose knowledge and get understanding that you might be fully who you were meant to be. The alternative is to die in ignorance like all the other ignorant persons of the world.

* * * * *

Jenny Berkeley, RN, CHN

66 Your body makes more serotonin when you get up early in the morning, typically at sunrise, and enjoy the sunlight all day. A bonus of having lots of serotonin is that you feel happier and tend to be more positive and have a calmer mental outlook.

**Jenny Berkeley, Nurse,
Certified Holistic Nutritionist, Author,
Magazine Publisher**

Personal Meditation

It's time to regain the habit of waking up early again. If you are not rising early it could be because you are sleeping too late at night. Reset your internal clock. Rise just before sunrise and enjoy your day. You'll experience a difference in your mind. And repeat this every day to improve your being. Think on it.

* * * * *

All three of these metals are needed by the body - copper for building enzymes, iron for blood cells, and zinc for nerve transmission, among other functions. You get them in the foods you eat. But it turns out that if you get too much of any of them, they can damage your brain cells. The difference between a safe amount and a toxic amount is surprisingly small.

**Dr Neal Barnard,
President, Physicians Committee for
Responsible Medicine**

Personal Meditation

We use metals in many aspects of our daily living. Yet, not many of us consider we might be over-exposed to them. Dr Barnard's point should encourage you to take account of how many metal objects interact with you daily. Meditate on the exposure and ways to reduce it in your life.

* * * * *

"What is the greatest gift you can ever give to yourself? The greatest gift you can give to your loved ones and to the world? It is the gift of deprogramming yourself. As we are successful in removing the toxic program that was injected into all of us from infancy, primarily through meals and food, we find our inherent joy, inner peace, creativity, radiant health, compassion, and spiritual clarity spontaneously returning.

**Dr Will Tuttle,
Author, World Peace Diet**

Personal Meditation

Now is the time of your awakening. In these moments of your life, all the paths have led to here. Give yourself a gift that begins in your mind. Choose to embrace curiosity and reject the bad programming that has seen a decline of your health and vitality.

* * * * *

❝ Today most people live in fear and confusion. We must have control over our emotions to be safe. The best way to gain control over your emotions is to live as closely as possible to our Creator's guidebook.

**Paul Nison, Author,
Health According to The Scriptures**

Personal Meditation

We are more than just a different kind of animal. We are living sentient human beings endowed with powers from our creator. Yet, we live in a world where confusion, fear, and deception is the norm. What you believe and what accept into your heart and mind will govern the outcomes in your life. Refuse to live in fear, confusion, and deception any longer. Grab a copy of our Creator's guidebook and start reading the simple truths in them.

Also, don't allows your emotions to be sucked in by memes on the internet or those 1 minute videos geared towards pulling at your emotions. Take time to unplug.

* * * * *

Whenever you doubt that you have the wisdom to do what is right, allow the spiritual to increase your optimistic imagination, which will ensure a viable option. Whenever caught up in the mundane patterns that are not enriching your heart, find what turns you on an utilize it until every action is generally heartfelt and authentic.

**Dr Brian Clement,
Co-Director, Hippocrates Health Institute**

Personal Meditation

Brian makes a very powerful point. Make all your actions heartfelt and authentic by connecting to the spiritual side of yourself. As a nurse and a champion for my patients, I let my love of them lead me. I laugh with them, cry with them, and be there for them. Many see me as an angel of light. I see myself as an ambassador of love and truth. Be that for others around you.

* * * * *

People are too concerned with what others will think or say about them. They dress themselves in new clothes, take lots of selfies to get the perfect one to post, and consult friends before responding to a tweet or text. This creates a stress level unheard of 50 or 100 years ago. There is no longer contentment in self and so discontentment abounds.

**Vaughn Berkeley, MBA,
Author, Human Rights Award Winner
Co-Publisher EternityWatch Magazine**

Personal Meditation

Are you living daily in a spirit of discontentment? Without contentment how can you have peace? You have to stop seeking approval from others. You are unique, beautiful, and whole being. Nurture peace and contentment within yourself in order to improve your mental outlook and mental health.

* * * * *

> My classmates often assumed I was mentally as well as physically disabled. They usually kept their distance unless I summoned the courage to strike up conversations in the lunchroom or in the hallway. The more I did this, the more they accepted that I really wasn't an alien dropped into their midst.

Nick Vujicic
Motivational Speaker, Author of Life
Without Limits

Personal Meditation

Nick's physical body was limited but his mind was perfectly fine. He recognized that shyness would keep him cut off from his peers because of their invalid perception of him. He broke through using love, friendliness, and being brave. You need to find that inner strength in you to be brave for those who love you in your life.

* * * * *

We all have within us that spark, that inner drive to become something great in this life. We have it in us to become champions of what is right. The stress, anxiety, dis-ease, and frustration that plague most people in their mind and in life, is because of a disconnect between who they are truly meant to be and who they are pretending to me. Be true to yourself. Live in truth and it will set you free.

* * * * *

Super Tip and Reminder

Do you know how lie detectors work? When people lie, it causes changes in the body. The blood pressure increases, their heart bests faster, their pupils dilate. This is the body naturally physically reacting to a disconnect between truth and lie.

In the mind, there are unmeasured factors like anxiety, fear, frustration, and the onset of dis-ease.

If you want to keep your mind and body healthy longer, the simplest way is to live in truth. Truth is the perfect alignment of what is reality with what is stated to be reality.

Quotes on Family Life

Chapter 8

* * *

The quotes in this section along with the personal meditation will help you to focus on the things in your life that are important. Family Life is a fundamental part of our existence on planet earth. As you read these and the meditation, take time to meditate on your own family life.

* * *

❝❝ The judge of a man's character is the manner in which he trains his children in life and in truth. It is the way in which he loves, nurtures, and cherishes his wife. It is the legacy he leaves behind in this world when he passes from it. This legacy must be established in truth, justice, and love.

Vaughn Berkeley, MBA,
Author, Human Rights Award Winner
Co-Publisher EternityWatch Magazine

Personal Meditation

Vaughn makes a point here about the higher ideals of life. These ideals are made manifest by our interactions with our family. Love, truth, and justice are some of the values which we live out in our lives and manifest in our world. Are you living your life in a way that brings love, truth, and justice into the lives of those who interact with you? If not, now is the time to make it happen.

* * * * *

I have worked with families whose children displayed language delay and emotional disorder with attention deficit. I focused on nutritional changes rather than use of medication. I asked for a five-day food diary and answers to a Health Questionnaire to better understand the problem and to gain increased understanding of the dietary history.

Karen Ranzi
Award Winning Author, Rawfod Coach,
Speech Pathologist, Section Chief at
EternityWatch Magazine

Personal Meditation

Karen has been a champion of a healthy family for decades. In her work with families she incorporates nutrition because healthy families need good nutrition. You need to make this a priority for your family.

* * * * *

I recommend to people who are just starting to make a drastic change in their diet to have a friend, family member, or professional counselor available so that they can talk through any issues that might come up from their healing crisis. Prayer is a great way to assist in the healing process, but it is also nice to be able to talk through some of the issues with someone.

Andrea Nison
Mother of two daughters, blogger, vegan

Personal Meditation

Andrea gives some great advice for anyone making a radical change in their diet. You may undergo a healing crisis. Have a friend or family member or a coach to talk to can help ease your fears, anxiety, and uncertainty.

* * * * *

❝ You family is an important part of your journey through dis-ease and into wellness. They can be a source of strength or a barrier of negativity. State your intention clearly and ask those who support you to be with you but love those who are not with you still.

**Jenny Berkeley, Nurse,
Certified Holistic Nutritionist, Author,
Magazine Publisher**

Personal Meditation

I've seen families shattered by dis-ease in hospital. The young wife by her husband side when told he has terminal cancer and not long to live. She wonders how she will raise their young children together. At times like these all difference must be set aside to nurture the one suffering and to take care of those who will be left behind. If you have a family member ill, be that support to them. If you are ill, tell them what you need from them.

* * * * *

❝ Honour thy father and thy mother: that thy days may be long upon the land which the LORD thy God giveth thee.

**Instruction from God to Moses
In the book of Exodus, Chapter 20, Verse 12
The Holy Bible, King James Version**

Personal Meditation

The holy scripture teaches children to love their parents because there is a promise of you will have time upon the land you were promised. For our modern life, we are still required to love and honour our parents because they need it. It brings to us a peace and comfort that come from God. Our lives are made better when we can help our parents lives be a little better. Sometimes this is a challenge with our parents but we should exercise patience, love, and compassion in that case.

* * * * *

[As a child] My family limited television viewing to very special programs, so we were creative in our play. Large boxes became playhouses and smaller boxes were preaching podiums or beds for our dolls, or even play stoves. The imagination is a powerful thing. The world of unlimited possibilities will unfold when a child learns to use his/her imagination

Joyce Harrell, RN, OCN
Health & Wellness Coach, Certified Vision
Board Coach, Aromatherapist.

Personal Meditation

Joyce mentions something that we need to nurture in children as well as in ourselves. It is out childlike imagination where be believe anything is possible. Revive your imagination in yourself and nurture it in your family.

* * * * *

> In that life-changing moment when I looked out and saw Daniel held above the crowd in that church, I realized that I'd become the miracle that I'd prayed for. God had not given me such a miracle. But he had made me Daniel's instead.

Nick Vujicic
Motivational Speaker, Author of Life Without Limits

Personal Meditation

Nick was 24 years old and speaking in a church. When he saw Daniel, a young boy with no arms or legs like him, it solidified Nick's divine purpose. Nick's parents met Daniel's parents and prepared them for all the struggle they would have to pass though raising a child with no limbs. They gave them hope for a better future for their son Daniel and for their family. You may be seeking a miracle but you may be someone's miracle and not realize it.

* * * * *

Our relationship to our parents is the second most important relationship we experience in our lifetime. It is one given to us at birth but one that begin nine months prior to our birth. For many of us, while we were still in the womb, we were loved by our parents.

**Vaughn Berkeley, MBA,
Author, Human Rights Award Winner
Co-Publisher EternityWatch Magazine**

Personal Meditation

Vaughn's point here is very important because many people go through life with unresolved feelings and issues with their parents. When their parents pass, there is a huge eruption of guilt, regret, and pain. Heal the relationship with your parents and your children now while you have time.

* * * * *

❝❞ As she [Jean Liedloff] watched the way the babies and young children were raised, she was amazed to see how in tune they were with their environment. Given almost complete freedom to explore their world, the children were not only intuitively cautious, they also became resourceful.

Lily Lanczi,
French to English translationor, freelance
writer, single parent

Personal Meditation

Lily wrote for us at EternityWatch Magazine many years ago. Her words offer us some insights into how important it is to allow our children to explore their environment safely in order to develop their full potential. It is for their spiritual, emotional, and mental health. Believe in your children.

* * * * *

" I've heard Dr Brian Clement say that when a person feels sad, just give a 3 or 4-year old a hug. Their overwhelming power of love and positivity will make everything else melt away. I've noticed this to be true with my children over the years. Grandparents need to spend time with their grand children.

**Jenny Berkeley, Nurse,
Certified Holistic Nutritionist, Author,
Magazine Publisher**

Personal Meditation

A sad thing I have noticed in North America is a disconnect between the elderly and their young grandchildren or great grandchildren. This should not be. We must do our best to foster this love between the older generation and the younger generation. There are health benefits to being among our children.

* * * * *

❝❝ Whoso robbeth his father or his mother, and saith, It is no transgression; the same is the companion of a destroyer.

**A Proverb in the book of Proverbs,
Chapter 28, Verse 24
The Holy Bible, King James Version**

Personal Meditation

Can a son or daughter rob their father or mother? Yes. They rob their parents of time, of love, of compassion, and of money. Good parents will give to their children out of their abundance of love. They hurt the most when selfish children only see them as a piggy bank. Love your parents. Do not rob them of the things which matter most in their lives. They are old and their life will end one day. In sickness, I see children become too busy to care for their ailing parents. This is a sadness I cannot describe. Change that by being love to your parents and to your children.

* * * * *

I was surprised to see how often my physical manifestations of pain and illness were actually caused by carrying others. As a mother, I took on the pain of my children. As an environmentalist, I took on the pain of our environmental degradation.

**Dagmar Schoenrock,
Author, Entrepreneur**

Personal Meditation

Dagmar was a Section Chief in the magazine for a year. She makes a good point here. Too many times we burden ourselves with the pain from other family members who do not desire change in their own lives. They only want to vent to us and return to their bad habits. It is important to help your family members change if you want to truly help them. Don't just be the person they vent to and then return to their bad ways. This is being their enabler instead of their true friend. It will make you manifest pain and illness when it is not aligned with who you are meant to be.

* * * * *

I love the holidays — especially the sharing of favorite foods that remind me of family and fond memories of childhood. How do I balance that with my raw vegan lifestyle? Easy! I prepare foods that are reminiscent of traditional holiday foods, using the best raw vegan ingredients possible, and I focus on creating the familiar flavors, textures, and appearance of foods that bring myself and my loved ones so much joy year after year.

Cherie Soria
Rawfood Chef, Author, Founder of the
Living Light Culinary Institute

Personal Meditation

Food reminds us of family times together. The sights and sounds of our familiar and comforting foods are pleasant to us. Families can try new recipes together. My parents had their first every vegan thanksgiving this year. I taught them how and we all ate it afterwards.

* * * * *

❝ I love you so much. Please forgive me for the pain and suffering I caused you. My life is blessed because of you. These sentences are ones that we should keep in our mind to soothe family bonds and heal the soul ties we create.

**Jenny Berkeley, Nurse,
Certified Holistic Nutritionist, Author,
Magazine Publisher**

Personal Meditation

Those three sentences I have mentioned can mean a world of value when used in the right moments. Families have conflicts because they are close to each other's hearts. The hurt is caused by bumps, bruises, and friction of being so close. Those sentences are like the grease in the wheel that keeps it moving smoothly. I have seen lives changed over the years by expressing the feelings in those sentences. I want the same love experience in your life.

* * * * *

> ❝ Humanity dodged a bullet with mad cow disease. Nearly an entire generation in Britain was exposed to infected beef, but only a few hundred people died. We weren't as lucky with swine flu, which the CDC estimates killed twelve thousand Americans.

Michael Greger, M.D.,
Author,
How Not To Die

Personal Meditation

Michael mentions something here that should cause you to sit up and think. Nearly an entire generation of people were exposed to a disease. That's mothers and fathers, uncles and aunts. Imagine if all your uncles and aunts along with your parents who are part of the same generation all died by the same disease. Imagine the terrible sadness and loss that would overshadow your life. Meditate on how you can help bring a healthier plant-based diet and lifestyle to your beloved family members.

* * * * *

"" Be patient, loving, and persistent with family members when teaching them about a healthier lifestyle. Given time, they will make steps to reach you if you remain true to the teachings you espouse.

**Jenny Berkeley, Nurse,
Certified Holistic Nutritionist, Author,
Magazine Publisher**

Personal Meditation

I've been trying for years to get my mom and dad to eat healthier and go on a plant-based diet. They made baby steps like trying an avocado for the first time, or trying a green smoothie. Finally this year, my mom and dad made the switch. For thanksgiving dinner, I did a cooking class and taught them how to prepare a delicious plant-based thanksgiving meal which they loved. They are now experimenting with their own recipes. Love and patience works but you must be a rock.

* * * * *

Family is one of your most valuable treasures on this planet. They can comfort you through your sickness and time of trouble. Sometimes they get on your last nerve. However, never foster hate towards your family. Forgive them if you need to. Love them as much as you can. Even if you disagree with them, you can still be like a river overflowing with love. They will see your example and you will be role model.

* * * * *

Super Tip and Reminder

No where is family more important that in the hospital environment. Remember, a hospital is a sanitized, drab, and dreary looking place. Sometimes it can feel cold and lonely. Having family with you brings warmth to your heart in those surroundings.

Remember Linda crying alone on her pillow after her breast removal surgery. In that movement she was truly all alone. No one should be alone like that.

Give you senior parents a call today and tell the you love them. Give your adult children a call and tell them you love them. Be there for each other. It is a source of healing for the heart and soul.

Quotes on Relationships

Chapter 9

* * *

The quotes in this section along with the personal meditation will help you to focus on the things in your life that are important. Relationships are not formed only with people. There are relationships to things we develop over time or to habits we develop. As you read these and the meditation, take time to meditate on your own life and relationships.

* * *

You become more like the people you associate with. Thus, you need to maintain relationships with people who care for you, lift you up, and do good for you. The better a relationship is for you, the better you become.

Vaughn Berkeley, MBA,
Author, Human Rights Award Winner
Co-Publisher EternityWatch Magazine

Personal Meditation

Vaughn makes an interesting point about relationships. Do you have toxic relationships in your life? Do you have friends who use you for their own benefit and never help you when you need it? Cut those people out of your life. They are toxic users and will cause you emotional pain and grief. For your own health and well-being find real relationships to build and nurture in your life.

* * * * *

> Those who loved me always encouraged me. They planted seeds in my heart. They assured me that I had blessings that could benefit others. Some days I believed them. Some days I didn't. But they never gave up on me.

Nick Vujicic
Motivational Speaker, Author of Life Without Limits

Personal Meditation

I love Nick's point. I've seen it in the medical field. I've seen it in my personal life I've seen it in my business life. I've seen people who believe in you more than you believe in yourself at times. They see the greatness in you that your momentary sadness or disappointment can't allow you to see. Thank God for those people. I'm also thankful whenever I am allowed to be that person for someone in my life whether it is a friend, a co-worker, a client, or a patient. Do you have people like that? Can you be that person for someone in your life? It will warm your heart.

* * * * *

When I met my husband I didn't think we had anything in common. When I got to know him, I knew he had a heart of gold under that rough exterior. It's like that with relationships in our lives. Take time to see if there is a deeper level you're missing.

Jenny Berkeley, Nurse, Certified Holistic Nutritionist, Author, Magazine Publisher

Personal Meditation

Sometimes we dismiss potential relationships with people because they look funny or they seem weird or are not pretty enough or some other superficial reason. Truth is, we are made for relationships. The people who are able to make true and authentic friendships with others by ignoring superficial things are the ones with the potential to fulfill their heart's desire. You should have a friend like that or be one like that.

* * * * *

I realized the relations between men and women have changed more in the past 30 years than they did in the previous 3000, and I began to suspect that a similar transformation was occurring in the role of marriage.

Stephanie Coontx,
Author,
Marriage, a History.

Personal Meditation

It seems like today marriages are a big source of stress to men and women. Stephanie that there is a shift in a way men and women relate to each other which is subsequently affecting the marriage relationship. It is possible to enrich your marriage to benefit you and your spouse. It takes time, patience, love, and strategy. Plus you must begin with hope. Hope that there is a possibility things will get better. Live in Hope today.

* * * * *

❝ I always tell my patients to eat the rainbow. Because every pigment in fruits and vegetables actually enters the nucleus of the cell and interacts with your genes, which is why it matters what you eat.

Dr Nalini Chilkov, L.Ac., O.M.D.,
Author, Clinician, Cellular Biologist

Personal Meditation

Nalini makes a point that we have been told for ages. You are what you eat. Now science backs this theory with proof. The phyto-nutrients in our foods of different colours help cells repair and function at the cellular level. The more rawfoods that are a variety of colours you consume, the greater variety of nutrients and phyto-nutrients you are giving your body. Now you need to look at your relationship to the rainbow of fruits and veggies available and how much of them you actually eat.

* * * * *

"People who are not successful in life have a lot of opportunities to achieve their goals and dreams. But they always find excuses like: I will start when I know everything; I will start when I have the money; I will start in 3 months when I have more time. Successful people know that if you're thinking like that you will never start.

Robert Rolih,
Speaker, Author, Event Manager

Personal Meditation

Robert is from Slovenia and has written for our magazine a couple of times. His words speak to your relationship with your true self. If you say you want success but make excuses then you don't really want it. If you say you want good health but make no effort then you don't. Maybe you feel unworthy of those things. You are worthy. Believe me, you are worthy. When you believe this, your relationship with yourself can go further than you could even imagine.

* * * * *

Kindness in words creates confidence. Kindness in thinking creates profoundness. Kindness in giving creates love.

Lao Tsu

Personal Meditation

If we could put the essence of this quote into one word, it would be relationships. When we use kindness in words, our words go to others to create confidence in them. When we use kindness in thinking , our thoughts dwell on how to make life better for those around us. And when we use kindness in giving, others receive with joy and thanksgiving. To be a great person begin with love and kindness in your heart. All your relationships which flow from those ideals will be good ones.

* * * * *

> Too many people live in a state of misalignment. They say they want this but are doing that. They eat bad but want good health. They support an industry that kills billions of animal yet say they love animals. They want truth but run towards pleasant lies.

**Jenny Berkeley, Nurse,
Certified Holistic Nutritionist, Author,
Magazine Publisher**

Personal Meditation

It makes me sad to see how many people are doing the opposite of what they say they really want. They seem to miss that point. You must wake up. You must become conscious of these things. Break free from the fog and find your relationship to truth. Be the true person you want to be in your mind by recognizing the gap between what you say and what you do. Eliminate that gap then you can be true.

* * * * *

" For every minute of anger, you will depress significantly and measurably the quality and quantity of your immune system. One minute of anger is six hours of [immune system] depression.

Dr Francisco Contreras, MD.
Oncologist, Surgeon

Personal Meditation

Francisco gives us a very interesting bit of information that more people need to know. Just one minute of anger can suppress your immune system for up to six hours. Your immune system is what fights disease from cancer to colds. The world and society is training people to be angry and to get angry. But people need to learn to be at peace and to be calm. How many times in a day do you get angry? Just one minute of anger is working against. Challenge yourself to be calm for en entire week.

* * * * *

> I was amazed at how quickly my health returned. I was completely healed in no time. The pain was gone. This led me to simplify all areas of my life.

Paul Nison,
Rawfood Chef, Author, Vlogger

Personal Meditation

Paul's testimony does sound amazing doesn't it. I want you to note something here. When he began to experience his healing, he changed his relationship to everything in his life. When he was no longer in pain, he was able to focus on his relationship with the things in his life. The things of his life were not adding value to his life but creating the stress he has become a prisoner of. When he was made free through healing, he rush forward to break the other chains in his life. I want you to look at your relationship to the things in your life. Are they your freedom or your prisons? Choose freedom.

* * * * *

When work is not aligned with what God has in mind for you, the work itself brings on stresses from every angle. There is no peace at the workplace, no peace when you leave the workplace, and no peace when you force yourself to return the next day.

Vaughn Berkeley, MBA,
Author, Human Rights Award Winner
Co-Publisher EternityWatch Magazine

Personal Meditation

Are you struggling in a job you hate? Are you putting up with it just because you have bills to pay? Vaughn's point is a good one. You need to align your work with the divine purpose for your life. A fish out of water will be stressed to death but in water it will thrive. Don't be the fish out of water. Find your place in the world where you fulfill your true purpose. It will take effort but it will bring you the most joy and fulfillment.

* * * * *

I went home, I got on my knees. I said, Father, you know the results of the test and everything. You're in charge, you created me; I am not going to have them cut up my face; I'm ready if you're ready - if its my time… give me the wisdom what I can do on my part so you can do your part.

Enoch DeBus
Cancer Survivor, Certified Nutritionist,
Gospel Worker

Personal Meditation

Sometimes, you need to pray the right prayer. Enoch had lived a full life. He took the gospel message all over the world. When he found out about the cancer on his face, he put his trust in God as he had done so many times before in his life. But Enoch prayed for wisdom to do his part so God can do his part. Are you willing to do your part for your health, wellness, and vitality? People choose a pill instead of a lifestyle change because of their stubbornness. Humility and obedience is what take you forward in grace.

* * * * *

Most dis-ease has its beginning in your gut. An unhealthy gut is the gateway for the various diseases people face in their lives. Heal the gut by doing what is right and the rest will work itself out.

Jenny Berkeley, Nurse, Certified Holistic Nutritionist, Author, Magazine Publisher

Personal Meditation

I am so passionate about a healthy gut that I wrote a book called, Colon by Design. I know that many diseases originate because people are not eating right, and pooping right. They are working against their body and the result is catastrophic diseases. I teach my clients about maintaining a healthy colon as I help them make healthy food and lifestyle choices. Good health is your birthright. Keeping it is your choice.

* * * * *

There is no easy walk to freedom anywhere, and many of us will have to pass through the valley of the shadow of death again and again before we reach the mountaintop of our desires.

**Nelson Mandela,
Human Rights Activist,
Former President of South Africa**

Personal Meditation

This is the last quote in this book but I saved the best for last. Life is a journey and we all see the mountaintop of our desired bur like Nelson says, we will have to pass through the valley of the shadow of death from time to time. Don't give up. Be faithful to your vision. Be true to your beliefs. And keep hope alive in your heart. Meditate on this as you think on your own life.

* * * * *

Love has been my driving force in everything that I do. I became a nurse because I have a love of people and care for their well-being. I became a magazine publisher because I wanted to let the world know of the good news I found in the rawfood diet. I take on select clients because I love people and recognize that some people need individual attention in order to get ahead. I've written numerous books and articles to share my wealth of knowledge out of love. Love is the extension of my relations with you, and all my fans and readers.

* * * * *

Super Tip and Reminder

Relationships are not a buzzword. They are one of the key components of a good life. Without good relationships in your life, you leave yourself open to depression, loneliness, sadness, despair, and other negative emotions. You can be surrounded by people and still be alone because there is no true relationship.

Always remember the truly important relationships in your life. Heal the ones that are broken. Strengthen the ones that are weak. Live your life with a focus on building better relationships.

You will benefit and those around you will benefit too.

A 99 Day Meditation Guide

Chapter 10

* * *

Day 1 to day 33: Focus on the Physical Part of Yourself

Silent Meditation: A silent meditation is one of the most beneficial things a person can do. While you think on the God of heaven and earth in the silence around you, you will begin to quiet your mind. Unfortunately in today's "always on" world, it is difficult to find that time alone. And this time is necessary long before you have a stressful situation. Try in the early hours of the morning, like 4 a.m. Do this every day for the first 33 days. Start with 5 minutes and work you way up to 60 minutes. It might be super hard at first because you are not used to being still but practice every day.

Prayer: Prayer is the way that believers communicate with the God of heaven and earth. Prayer is talking to God. You are engaging your heart and your mouth. When you practice to discipline these two things, you will begin to grow in your physical realm of existence.

Exercise: Exercise is one of the better physical comfort tools you can use. It has numerous beneficial impacts on the body, both physically and mentally. Exercise like walking helps a person to focus on other things instead of their own worries. Exercise has also been shown to reduce stress, depression, and feelings of being sluggish. Exercise also boosts the "happy hormones" produced by the body. It brings more oxygen into the body and helps to move toxins around and out of the body. A nice, brisk walk will also help with bowel movements as the impact of gravity and your feet pounding the floor helps the stool to move.

Warm Bath: This is another excellent way to comfort yourself instead of reaching for comfort foods. A nice, warm bath where you just relax and soak almost feels like your troubles are soaking away. It is great when you have the time and need to de-stress. If you use some of your favourite scented oils, you can make the experience even better. When you are in a bath, you won't be thinking of any comfort foods.

Use 33 Quotes from this book to Guide on Days 1 to 33: You will pick out 33 verses that you will use to help you focus during your first 33 days. I could tell you but your heart will be a better guide. You will find you will pick the quotes which you need for those days. Write the page numbers for the quotes below so you can keep to your plan.

1_____ 2_____ 3_____

1_____ 2_____ 3_____

1_____ 2_____ 3_____

1_____ 2_____ 3_____

1_____ 2_____ 3_____

1_____ 2_____ 3_____

1_____ 2_____ 3_____

1_____ 2 _____ 3 _____

1_____ 2 _____ 3 _____

1_____ 2 _____ 3 _____

1_____ 2 _____ 3 _____

Day 34 to day 66: Focus on the Mental Part of Yourself

Talking With Your Spiritual Partner: Most people don't recognize that they have a spiritual partner on their journey. While children are growing up, their spiritual partners are their parents, or uncles, or aunts, who are helping them understand more about their relationship to God. As adults, it may be a spouse, partner, boyfriend, or girlfriend who takes on that role.

Optimism: Optimism is believing that the world is a better place. When some people eat chocolate they might believe the world is a better place, but that is only until the biochemical reaction of the chocolate wears out. A better and more permanent way to keep that view is by purposely being optimistic. By looking for good in the world, in people you know, and in yourself, you can position your mind to be optimistic about life.

Aroma Therapy: This is another way to help soothe your mind. Using your sense of smell to fill your mind with pleasant aromas is great. I would not recommend any synthetic chemicals. Use fresh flowers, or the smell of fresh fruit, or even oils made from plants.

Warm Bath: This is another excellent way to comfort

yourself instead of reaching for comfort foods. A nice, warm bath where you just relax and soak almost feels like your troubles are soaking away. It is great when you have the time and need to de-stress. If you use some of your favourite scented oils, you can make the experience even better. When you are in a bath, you won't be thinking of any comfort foods.

Use 33 Quotes from this book for Days 34 to 66:
You will pick out 33 verses that you will use to help you focus during these next 33 days. I could tell you but your heart will be a better guide. You will find you will pick the quotes which you need for those days. Write the page numbers for the quotes below so you can keep to your plan.

1_____	2_____	3_____
1_____	2_____	3_____
1_____	2_____	3_____
1_____	2_____	3_____
1_____	2_____	3_____
1_____	2_____	3_____
1_____	2_____	3_____
1_____	2_____	3_____
1_____	2_____	3_____
1_____	2_____	3_____

1_____ 2 _____ 3 _____

Day 67 to day 99: Focus on the Spiritual

Bible Verse Meditation: The holy scriptures are filled with verses that help to quiet the mind and comfort the soul. For example, "yea though I walk through the valley of death, I shall fear no evil, because you are with me," or "love your god with all your heart, this is the first great command, and the second is like it, love your neighbour as you love yourself."

Affirmations: Affirmations are statements that you repeat to yourself or in the presence of others to help you position yourself mentally for the day or the challenge ahead of you. Affirmations are very effective. These short lines signalled that the person saying it was ready for action. And saying it before taking action was the affirmation. But there are also affirmations used in everyday situations like the student who tells herself, "I'm so ready for this exam" or the student who says "I am ready to win this game." Even professional sporting athletes use affirmations before a game to motivate themselves. If the military, movies, and students use affirmations, then there is something valuable to their use. Use them for the next 33 days when you focus on your relationship to God.

Use 33 Quotes from this book for Days 67 to 99:
You will pick out 33 verses that you will use to help you focus during these 33 days. I could tell you but your heart will be a better guide. You will find you will pick the quotes which you need for those days. Write the page numbers for the quotes below so you can keep to

your plan.

1_____ 2_____ 3_____

1_____ 2_____ 3_____

1_____ 2_____ 3_____

1_____ 2_____ 3_____

1_____ 2_____ 3_____

1_____ 2_____ 3_____

1_____ 2_____ 3_____

1_____ 2_____ 3_____

1_____ 2_____ 3_____

1_____ 2_____ 3_____

1_____ 2_____ 3_____

* * *

About The Author

Jenny Berkeley is a registered nurse, a certified holistic nutritionist, a health educator, raw food chef, and best selling kindle author. Jenny is one of Toronto's most connected individuals in the living foods movement. She has worked both locally in Canada and internationally. She is a tiny gal with a big heart that she wears on her sleeve. Jenny has over 25 years of experience in the medical profession caring for her patients, being their advocate, and supporting her colleagues.

In addition to her busy schedule as a medical professional, Jenny still finds the time to do television interviews, radio interviews, and even speak to heads of government on behalf of the organic and living food movement. She goes boldly for the benefit of all Canadian, young and old. She is an author, speaker, lecturer, and blogger. Her Twitter following is over 35,000. She is also the co-founder and publisher of EternityWatch Magazine, Canada's magazine dedicated to the vegan and raw-vegan community. Her magazine is focused on holistic health and every issue promotes a holistic approach to health by looking at diet, lifestyle, and your environment. Every issue includes a plant-based recipe for the readers to enjoy. The magazine reaches over 120,000 people each quarter;

Her website, Eating4Eternity.org is a wonderful resource for the health-minded that covers topics ranging from square-foot gardening to the living foods.

Facebook: jen.berkeley | Twitter: sproutqueen
Instagram: sproutqueen

Email: info@eating4eternity.org

Amazon Author Page:
http://www.amazon.com/Jenny-Berkeley/e/B00761ML3A

Look for more great titles from The Holistic Health Nurse SeriesTM
www.eating4eternity.org/hhns/

* * * * *

More from CM Berkeley Media Group

CM Berkeley Media Group, based in Canada, works with its authors to produce books which help to uplift the human spirit, spread the message of health and wellness, and offer practical insights in finances, and other areas. We also offer services to help authors convert their books to Kindle or ePUB format, get their book edited, and get a great cover design, and other services for independent authors.

Facebook Fan Page: cmberkeleymediagroup
Website: www.cmberkeleymediagroup.com
Email: info@cmberkeleymediagroup.com

Check out other great titles from our authors

For Adults

Eating4Eternity: Unlock Your Holistic Health Lifestyle.
Amazon Link >> http://amzn.to/1cO0kFd

Sweet Raw Desserts: Life Is Sweet Raw™
Amazon Link >> http://amzn.to/19msz2E

Can I Offer You A Cigarette: The Only Sure Way To Break The Smoking Habit
Amazon Link >> http://amzn.to/1enAfiJ

Colon By Design: Overcoming The Stigma Of Colon Sickness And Unlocking True Colon Health™
Amazon Link >> http://amzn.to/JGH05a

Fresh Food4Life™: The Case For Taking Back Control of Your Food And Empowering Your Family And Community.
Amazon Link >> http://amzn.to/J9yrQF

For Teens and Young Adults

The Youth Leadership Empowerment System™
Try out the FREE mini-course for youth.
Amazon Link >> http://amzn.to/1hRtMPy

For Children

The adventures of Moshe Monkey and Elias Froggy book series.

The Adventures of Moshe Monkey and Elias Froggy: A Healthy Business (Volume 1)
Amazon Link >> http://amzn.to/18V4NKO

Moshe and Elias Build A Garden (The Adventures of Moshe Monkey and Elias Froggy) (Volume 2)
Amazon Link >> http://amzn.to/1cj7elb

Moshe and Elias Tropical Vacation (The Adventures of Moshe Monkey and Elias Froggy) (Volume 3)
Amazon Link >> http://amzn.to/1hb1py7

For more great info from the author, fun activities for your children, and more, visit: http://mosheandelias.com

* * * * *

Want to become a published author in 90 days? CM Berkeley Media Group has an online training program to help anyone aspiring to achieve this dream. Find out more about it and realize your dream at
http://cmberkeleymediagroup.com/writeyourbookin90days/

Already have your manuscript written and want to work with us to turn your book into a kindle reality? We have services to help you polish your work, design the cover, and get your book formatted for kindle and print too. To get started visit our website at http://www.cmberkeleymediagroup.com

Great Resources

EternityWatch Magazine (www.eternitywatchmagazine.com)

EternityWatch Magazine is the premier magazine for those seeking a truly holistic approach to health and wellness. The magazine is founded on the belief that good health is everyone's birthright and that by proper education, people can make the right choices to maintain their good health. The magazine is focused on plant-based nutrition, thus it caters to the rapidly growing vegan, and raw/living foods movement. You can get it free online just by signing up for it.

Eating4Eternity.org (www.eating4eternity.org)

Eating4Eternity is founded by Jenny Berkeley and is focused on her personal coaching approach. On the site, you will find news articles on health and wellness, Jenny's blog posts with her personal insights into what is happening in the medical field, paid courses and webinars, and some free information.

88Deals4U.com (www.88deals4u.com)

This site is an online hub for North Americans looking for great deals. With 88Deals4U.com, you'll find deals that are $.88 cents or deals that are $88. They love 88 over there. You can save as much as 50% off items you'd pay a lot more elsewhere. For the small membership fee of $24 per year, it is worth it.

Berkeley Academy (http://berkeley.academy)

This Canadian online hub breaks from the mould of traditional universities and colleges. The courses are not geared to get you a job but to help you live a life of worth. Conventional schools don't teach this material because it's not profitable for them.

FreshFood4Life.com (www.freshfood4life.com)
Fresh food for life is part of living a healthy life. This website has information about a revolutionary garden solution for the home owner with no space. You can view videos, articles and order your own garden system. You can grow 24 crops in you very own kitchen. I have one of these and so can you.

**Hippocrates Health Institute
(www.hippocratesinst.org)**
Hippocrates Health Institute is the premier institute for alternative health and wellness. With over 50 years of experience in educating people to take control of their health destiny, the institute has a solid foundation. Their website talks about their programs, plus you can find copies of their magazine.

**CM Berkeley Media Group
(www.cmberkeleymediagroup.com)**
This is the publisher website where we also publish short articles on trends in the industry. Our long standing online course on how to write your book in 90 days is now offered through the academy but you can still learn more about it on this site as well as purchase copies of digital books.

* * * * *